FLEDGE

A Phenomenology of Spirit

FLEDGE

STACY DORIS

A Phenomenology of Spirit

NIGHTBOAT BOOKS

CALLICOON, NEW YORK

to Rayzl, Laish Gedalya, and Chet

This book stands for

a) a close translation of Hegel's *Phenomenology of Spirit*

b) a mainly at arm's length appropriation of some poems by Paul Celan

these being two extremes in language of

c) a log of disasters

d) a register of miracle

e) also this is a bunch of love poems of undying love

Except for flexibly taken compounds, there are mostly no two-syllable words in this book of six-syllable lines. The attempt is to push musicality-duration and naively literalize nonduality.

These poems are continuous. But because there are swells and hillocks, rough sections can also be imagined, for example:

A section beginning with the poem beginning "Please bee get my hands I" and ending with the poem beginning "To count's our horizon" (pages 1-27)

A section beginning with the poem beginning "Since time melts down to jumps" and ending with the poem beginning "Our throat dressed, celebrate" (pages 28-57)

A section beginning with the poem beginning "To sink to a field warm" and ending with the poem beginning "This starts in emptying" (pages 58-90)

Please bee get my hands I
want my hands back I love
you – so time's gone? Rind's tight
that means no time's not want
churns don't eat don't want calls
give to grab, extended

I'm organizing clean
myself in myself lured
so long as there's no sticks
only flux, teeth known as
waves and the rest. Nothing
the glue in which lungs all
dip, a glass folds your names

Why I won't sleep yet or
so we train for that one's
marbling her head flat
from this glass will not stop
must stay kept apart, mill
twoness the fork of lie

down now its tines blow us
in hey we bent up these
these tines for rolling let's
roll no let's not roll there

Let me just slide this up
then launch the bed in muck
let him have it alone
as the half and the half
half why we built this we're
gone now to our shell game
on our boat that runs fixed

They're rumbling the strings
of my house is your house
see you said that so long
if true then I don't have
a house somebody pounced
on the gateway through weeds
days which is my house if
I leave now you know since
I'm the milk of all cats
which time one and still me

Since we train to keep up
for certainty though rope
through ropes so branch or lunge
then all the twist of hairs
anything can flat my
interest make rope what
rope is crumbs pulled or fast
battery I slid off

I see you try to do
what I do exactly
I do exactly what
only in so far as you
try because one act pops
its braid for which we train
clean up the box the kids
the creek clean up the stage

Our dough mix sang as mine

my own crop flew new ones

ow it won't hurt I just

just puffed it out your feet

so we train to bolt up

but that everywhere cracks

as me, including fruits

belong in oxygen

and such. I know wake up

I'm gonna wear my shift

To squat for bright globe pails
as wind pet finch seethes dust
or rock so your shine won't
scrape if I move you are
the one who moved while shut
my hands back from once you
wear a hat I grow out

So before asking which
is want or want so vast
it licks my horse myself
shine my horse a goldfinch
in footfalls as useless
to fill you yourself burst

tufts seed no not a real
one a horse my myself
in reorder as tight
wipes through the grass now of
this my hammering my

This is my store of pears
branched it fell down a few
placed stains a dappling
beat beat when I beat you
beat me exactly if
owl spins an exactly
grooved ledge, end of I saw

The load of load of all
steps off it must weight yours
in as far as mine so
not marked, just a whole dash
a drawer between my stool
and my stoop that shifts down

your look with my eyes on
accounting grouse there goes
nothing in me but there
through you now stacks you what
I see you do I do

STACY DORIS

Docked one as both fledged move
the sole of its kind. Cough
notices, it co-airs
refreshment, I splash from
you again, each end clocks
its own seams, mere train wound
and full skip to the wrought
push-off a layering
azalea and spread
if one half coin and this.
No. One half coin and this

I grab your pants since you
ate up the coverings.
Your pants sound wide of grape
when you see grab my pants
but with your teeth we are
identically these cloths
then safe, so I that I don't
want to be safe again

Come look at my tip my
tip makes noise my tip makes
this noise inside of it
this broke part you rope to
scrape you all outside still
when you grab as touch drowns
ant circles they flocked count
of strung through roars and posed
done with you I have shells

I make my hat in your
dumpling unripened
shoot, fig on pack, that cut
if bare's an abstraction
I'm your shirt, not drawn
that's just my bluebird head
got stuck you can come tie it

Strung our underneaths hit
where since you're not outside
me, I won't clump you in
the box extinguish. We
hold what we own so light
it balls where ball isn't
some act one of breeze just

play across a grained edge
in you droop from me
my toes wilt if I suck
if you suck pickling
your smile, the long bulb,
massed, cat in a huge
field of wheat it folds up

I want what you want in
your want of it, but what
we want isn't the same.
A strain of rows then, us
thread so we determine
I'll take everything you
slurp up the drip offs, plus
you can watch. Everything
means wraps and envelopes,
you get the productions,
gloss pocks of minerals

As you go ripe I smooth
as you get ripe she'll make us
pluck full but fluent then
castaway spaghetti
spaghetti has two names
french fry and bowtie if
they're not done unbox me
if not done so permanent

Because we don't make we're
kin to permanent what
we touch, I most you then
by toes, by not pass off
wafts ouch-inches up from
the carpeting, their plants
or the loom of your smell
is my mouth, unsteady
swarmed with infections
we jiggle, obstinate
to the little night: "Take"

Air's hold on air, edge gone
for outskirts, televised
up. Not as viewpoint not
as swarm we infiltrate
but stuff in our mouths makes
us loft, nooks and cardboard
sink of warm and needless
patterning, note's downside
before we trained to skim.
So nice looks won't stop us
but wind does, I drink it
it seeps through your nothing's
more trumpeted part

If I can't sleep you can't
sleep and that's a walkway
the tune when-I-see-you-
(first in the morning)—smile

We must be the big thing
ladling itself with
itself in your bright coats

opposing the pond keeps
set not contingently
nor contingent as we
sugar-coat time since looks
creep up the chocolate
the chocolatey stems

Take your two hands and push
the weight of your face on
my face a commotion
to reach the unfolding
that flood and don't count it

you see yourself just as
when you've twice lost the pit
toe bursts off to "I need"
for example in the
rain I need my cardinals

If ears bloom we bring crumbs
or fingertips that hoard
confetti (a thought said
my face throws you into
hiccupping) if I give
you this I am stamped or
want to show you my hands
I eat when I can keep
them uncurling my knees
to join so what you tell
I can tell for now hurts

For example this rain's
an example how in-
stead of to feel what we
feel are hillsides. Instead
of race what we feel nudged
to cracks with the upshot

of sand. Aside from sweet
potatoes and bread there's
nothing I like more than
our straps unless I know
you like it. I grab to
make sure you want it more

To count's our horizon
we train ourselves on wind
hold clips our hands at squares
with to reach not an edge.
Shape's what we could forge

but we move, move and crash.
We're see-through, gaseous,
a ball trips our hard side.
We turn up. Lengthening
you grab all my colors
lengthening I let you

Since time melts down to jumps
we don't count out, don't walk
and switch with discomfort
between sleep and awake.
Don't understand the wait
yet take turns. With no shift
comes no pictogram no
end. On sand we separate
flat from arc, twist the brink
of agreement. A bowl
on the gangplank won't match
its figs, but a branch may.
Our faces swell of love
the rest's a raft of noise

STACY DORIS

Formerly we combed owls.
They oriented us
with nobody to guess
and now we can't either.
They're surf now. Or a mouse,
if visible, must pair

light. A web, crooks. Then they
fold us in terrific
balls after which we trip
and bang just like to soar
can tear the grass into
a here and a "here"

Touch says you are for my
touch. I cling feet first, feet
then hands legs arms necks head
with my tongue in reverse
always stiffer, readied.

Since we break things to shreds
since we clip and spit them
we tarnish awareness.
But since acts are all love
nothing stops our fingers

If I turn to you I
turn in. We blow up
time with additional forks,
devastate companions
kayaking out, forecast
doneness with a trail. Get
lost in light with the jabs
each step on stilts: work tub
stuck in jump, so the numb
pinch of each dip weighs twice
velveted and here's here

The difference between you
and for example my
arm is not made. My hairs
your hold on light, my spine
your hunched entirety

of fun. There are no paths,
just openly we've
still electrified the pond,
one shock per kingfisher

Your breath is for my hand
to grab like foals or ice
needlessly lead to rungs
and while each mass your hair
my unbounding my step
when it hurts do I tell
I'm left, or determine
we're the same in my cut
drink you off in its waves

My pain – hold me my pain –
hold me my pain – yank yank
hold me now the first x
feet past my eye's all fog
and I can't hone them hold
me giantly top jays their
tongues loom on anyone's
arm to the world to norms
I undo the bloom so
you can change the nectar

STACY DORIS

Toes mean sight mean dove called

decided decided

spans a community

of whims, a whole sink pole

a whole overall lawn

entertained. As it turns

out swan's disunity

of heart sides: a boat town

thrashed of here, entire

Can be named my kid 'cause
a drop, full (in the x
space of blur are small hairs
I snip in providing)
hilarity you then
thread back your head, teeth blow
correction momentous
so animals don't fall
we need a sweet toe line
animals can't fall in

Eyes interfere or sight's
exploded a gift, pit
then recognizing ends.
If I were you my life

would be almost my eyes,
your life's almost my eyes.
Sleep and stare soothe the same
blueberry don't you cry

As my eye pulls each dip
magnetic or fish line
spoke of fold as fold spoke,
as much as a walled us
up and down my big spoon
awaking buzz I dash
through what rides me – what you
don't stir but magnify
slide me in a half so
my walk won't register
as advancing you keep
track of your hair in bursts

Move this compassing or
thorn that just runs through me
ball how can I show the
effortless blew up my
own secretly drained of
where you don't know beach balls
so that when you walk we
toss the blue fast up there

Hey look at hey I love
It I love it I love
I love it I'll make it
even beautifuller

What I hold in my hand
which is just now flies more
glad and yours veined to sky
call so that when you leave
I miss but patch and bolt.

When I'm back knock knock who's
no all rocks have a sap
have a sap in them there

You may hug me but your
trajectory's roughed up
and so beats, unsounded
but mine refilters more
than me to me, you give.

If you call I don't hear
and in the crescendo
mold grown most in arm's reach
prance the more whole from sleights
impassible up back
in runs and starts a place
you can't fill with your mouth

I come close but I won't
think there's a far or feel
it, that's philosophy,
a built-in don't know drop
slims with our fingerings
and glides but you won't fall
though for me to fall's up
a romp or plot you drink
then I'm left, then I try
to swing out through rock's webs
and am caught, twist in there
now the fact of blue can't
tow me, want, want a way

What winds tight and whirls you
carve it an alarm you're
in charge while I leech in
what you shed then won't skim
my flaked reach, waste of now
let's get out of this skunk's
house, out of this old noise

I do not shed. I fall
up but not loud as you
look a moth salts this glass
to territories to
wave back, to see with
all its stark arteries
in which we're cleared out to
a purity of traps
where our small bee won't die
just shine with do it too

We're occupied, indoors
frittering a midge and
flattery which snags on
hare's skin wind. Where a wing
marks her, dust inked, wave me
too, dressed in crows, where names

crumb, so we're separate
and so ornamental,
in thrones to sing round, what
else, entangled no place
scours irregular
garbed as what's left out next

Stems, us – which polishes
and lifts out to the cold
we see but I won't see
me clipped from you, my needs
so flood the room with their
unhearing through your laugh
that pulls me once I step.

Talk is the pool where part
has no parts, play in sink.
We catch your stems in bowls
ram with our full arms.
The spot between pond and
to know it pools hums once

Since I love I fall down
since a ridge is all that
disintegrates so home.
And firs bind this which won't
add dust. Hold my hand or
else I won't walk. Since space
is not imagining
it's not navigable
not implicit so gives
so we fight for one and
lose, then the "cupped" can eat
me as I watch you dance

Since realization's
nourishment, I won't speak
so that you fill me with
remodeling guess each
wing as independent.
Each moth's licorice so
I save them, bendable
investigate in tongue

Bright as contrasted with
bright that explosive said
hurl volcanically bright
so large when crumbling
activate small mud wisp
ineffably mud wisp
to tent the intrusion
which is as there's no cart
from ripe and rot, just treats
of ice I lick there's no
point, just feathering plus
what I want to get what
I want while we give out

Thrown into rain, with dogs
crops and spits, unlining
gunk which then owns me one
life, through claws, through noise cupped
ostentation as scratch
so far I'm your walk now

I'll walk off this huge plack
of lawn, why not? Why if
it's to reach that why since
our braid roots obscenely,
floods down the wonderment

To wipe entireness
its fault in stick with crushed
hewn then my flip point
doll or duck whose end ties
to you trickley jams
the bud part erasing
with its fake lens named "hug"
and endlessly sift out
and feels its ballooning's
ballooning overall

Hold's unanimous broom
to the point one-sided
I bang my fun shoots worse,
high. Then I want the pile

which refuses yet jerks
magnetic seats could comb us
in a four-hour life
my lustrous packs what
you since chewed up as gum
as gum it must own souls

This one-sided self-sealed
day acts like no more fun
in my fun in a fit

and repudiation's
choice, atmospheric I
may case my sweet theft's sigh,
suspension permanence

Without your hands I can't
walk, so flung drops in drops
slow from wet wove kiss
me constructions you at
least plunged as from a burn

you as a state of touch
for demolished, to laugh
face to face puzzling
solidity I bang
your head as merriment
overall sourness
sand-eating won't dispel.
It rounds, glassed to the mirth
of your hands tear from your
hands all its weight on up

Then you as my outside,
which tears federation,
law, fun and possibly
beat you best inhabit
which wave now pokes you off
so I turn honeying

Our throat dressed, celebrate
hinged the wing to I split
cupped at both when the half
from the half of split builds
a leaf falls up the thrush
for lost care in its curl
aka purrs bounds skies
or what's in our reach comes

To sink to a field warm
not dragonfly where if
hung there can you get to
ask everything to ask
for both? If not or stilled
can you get everything
save for both in asked where
the rope of me by me

coin to sink to a fence
if warm there can you get
both down at the sweet mart
in everything asked for
can you get everything
crosslegged on the stairs
for both in asked with oars

A warmth hugs actual
warmth in skeined occurring
since occurring. What pours
filled with rocks pours still with
late songs, the rarity
of want to stay. Or
if I recoil me
for smeared jam in my nose
come do that to my house

Clarity smears me, kin
to why that rag at each
dip shows its arrival
as clogged, as come to veins
dived more incidental
than roots root velveting

Suspending's suspension
which rag, all elastic
unbursting no get back
unopened let's do it
so full we perched in dark
we hands baled the lake droves
we paid it in grape coins

Face, light, milk grit, air skins
skin. My mouth stain ripped through
in the loamed slow of all
moves, too velveted sweep
the grape froth coats you, whipped
tinge of cloth out to sift
a fluency plays us
struck and not struck barbells
crash with our oars and heat
layering's velveted

So that all I edge sticks
to the peel's sweet new bark
though you slip in the way
rocks, give. Gratitude lands
what I entertain lost
its tuft as mirroring
cupped it in my jaws, rock
as long cat so I swarmed
unrebellious, I kissed
shoes in a feast of laws

Where the sky launched this thrush
to my call, a cat strikes
rocks to my call I name
strands through your song I-know
I-know I-know I point
and name myself not took

to be rocked, then sweep me
if not mouthed you flood with
yourself but I need to
sound each particular

Bird laps, not rearranged
so air rearranges
all spots, cat, glass does sound
weight each? Is to tell each
my way to hold me an-
other, if another

My voice dispenses you
to yourself a goldrush
of scratch you in growl in
place by accidental
mood all security
from spooned well its snapshot
overlooks the insides

Besides the pocks in rain
I can lend you this fake
this snag, yours, wet, bound clipped
my bottomless full chance
snaps in the caves in know's
bestiary pull
by sounds, in flattery's
big seat collection smoothed

Tied down so not cast off
my bruise, a takeover

if I occupy this
spot, my toy's discomfort
my cat won't freeze her pleat
my bug won't prod judgment
and so twice I'm the both

STACY DORIS

Chasing a grunt to know
twists me when you're held in
each, a pail you can't wear
wind clamps the waves all we
remember is fun with
time's not identical

My neck makes another
holds you where it points me
chipped, hummingbird, straws build
this spree, brushed undoubling

we braid. My cup of names
takes my heel as an oar
the raft actually growls

Your name or mine so drew
my flake ripe the sand crashed
a one bubbling gone

to find's purposeless flute
I especially hem.
Yes yes we two snort, dance
the mouse jig, it is, it
is through a flag my horse

pried so I'm the horse now
I'll take you off my ear

Horse that's me grows. It zooms
and cartwheels. If I'm in me
next, this twine if I bend
I'm still far from I want
bubbling general
bubbling fished in you
for me, "midst" in terms of
a "potato," the hill
of wind's sameness that grazed
each saw especially
etched each grape permanent

Bubbling sold all grounds
by rips from bubbling
wrung, clothed. Hold or a cat's
sounds bubbling leaves leave
your hold, in its same ramps
pinprick's ingredients
a cloud of your eyes broth
tint kissed in their way cats
precisely untangle,
grip in the lake of what
clump might be including
if it were including

Including flick and crop
a low hum through waxwing
plied, the rill of some chime
or continent in twists
leaf and leaf, single-hand.
Your eyes pump sounds in their
bowls of commodity
twine while I stack this house
in to water the rain

STACY DORIS

Your eyes dig up the flakes
run pitch through a drone's curls
to spoon it. The "o" grip
whose hold unmoors our fly,
their crocuses, my road.
Since I cramped the forks I'll
go there to replant them

A green plush veins our oars
in the wide none of "no."
Now you call mouse what jacks
still a rag so I clip
it bright. Grab and smooch on.
I stuff her in your mouth,
this now animal. This
crease I love, want to swim
with him to soak him through
mud and then slip to feed

Pail means sound has its place
but if I hinge a bird
anywhere I must trot
my rag toward it furl you
to coast up the scraps and
their gleam and tickling

dash my rag velveted
robs us in bubbling
loops caved dark cascade-fulls
oxygen's oxygens

To shed "goods" rind ajar, cub
full swarm to my blue rag,
its thread, shared milks pour out
laugh grasps twoness curve best,
in the bubbling we
sand match with twist, eyesight
where clouds tap their churned dive
gibberish, froth a base

You sort each tick from each
primped for allegiance, how
twoness pecks us a ripe
frivolity's heart you
lean on that the great cake
of underneath starts us
can we sip ignoring
the wet part? To find out

I throw everything from
me and watch it surge back
to my hands plus my rag
so what's inanimate
screws flamed off easily

"Rag," since names blot scraps home
magnetic. I catch walls
in its rush, reel it back
everything jumps into
my pillowcase while you
hinge each step to the last
one's crust forked through their mouse
huffs that sort air from air
that turns back a nick once

You roll in own I give
since I want you to pack
to note your hold you don't
want to own. This braids us
in drafts of the swing's
leaves where you want me up

everything strips it round
to music we'll eat your
dress stacked on my waitlist
you know how to line down
the time and its firebrand
inextinguishable

Comes from "know" or useless,
we recircuit tap, its
strenuous fix lifts though
agreement unseats us
decorative and bogged
the gills of everything
as dress, as owls, so we
bale a front porch in glee

STACY DORIS

With my rag I play mouse
is stuck the mouse is stuck
down behind the armoire
I can't get her mouse mouse
mouse ut-oh slid part through

my lips from yards you curl
not drown by your rags lump
in a count: dog bear fish
all must be hugged hard once
each rag particular
more than we undertow

So we bring them to cage

honeysuckle let slide

know itself more than we

know so we pulse at once

in and out while the dips

coax your mouth sealed and mine

chimes, prehensile, whole

curlicue-paved, sails on

There visible a praise
burns us and the rag
sniffs from our hands we foal
our rag and say so's
additional just flicked

In galloping I fold
quit my hinge and pounce, fish
where everything's a hug:
cigarette butts rinds caps

you a swept regardless
clang of vines, grape, rose hitch

To spin carves rooms. Color
pinks. Recognizing shade
you point to your face. "Shade,"
you sing out to make sure
it won't skip. When our shades
skip we hug them to bits.
That scrapes gravity off
see through just for me now

So your hands leak you store
them, so your lips break to
strings. So when you hang mashed
clematis, quick twigs spin
tall ears. Play ends when two
shapes are forced to match, drop

If a can rolls in wind
we go songless or dull.
We lose the can or rag

to watch it roll in wind
left repeating turned out

so that we know where touch
separates and may build
the afternoon in sips

This starts in emptying
the crate: "dump, dump." The words
cart away as in "pink"
or "bulge." Uplifting the
mouse-rag buzzed drips to glass
our climb in big sized shoes.

The mouse rag as much in
immediacy as
immediacy shreds

to mouse-rags, a puff bath
this panoply called door
the general float crowns

ISBN: 978-1-937658-04-5

Design and typesetting by HR Hegnauer

Text set in Bell

Cover art by Rayzl Doris-Wiener and
    Laish Gedalya Doris-Wiener

The publisher would like to thank Yedda Morrison
and Chet Wiener for their invaluable help with
this publication.

Cataloging-in-publication data is available
From the Library of Congress

Distributed by University Press of New England
One Court Street
Lebanon, NH 03766
www.upne.com

Nightboat Books
Callicoon, New York
www.nightboat.org

Stacy Doris (1962-2012) wrote seven books of poetry in English: *Kildare* (1995), *Paramour* (2000), *Conference* (2001), *Knot* (2006), *Cheerleader's Guide to the World: Council Book* (2006), *The Cake Part* (2011), and *Fledge: A Phenomenology of Spirit* (2012). She is also the author, in French, of *La Vie de Chester Steven Wiener écrite par sa femme*, (1998), *Une Année à New York avec Chester* (2000), and *Parlement* (2005). She is co-editor of two anthologies of French poetry in translation: *Twenty-two New (to North America) French Poets*, with Norma Cole (1997) and *Violence of the White Page, Contemporary French Poetry in Translation*, with Emmanuel Hocquard (1992). Her translations, from French, include: *Everything Happens* by Dominique Fourcade (2001), *Tracing* by Ryoko Sekiguchi (2003), and *Christophe Tarkos: Ma Langue est Poetique--Selected Work*, with Chet Wiener (2001). She lived in New York, Paris, and San Francisco, where she taught in the Creative Writing Program at San Francisco State University.

NIGHTBOAT BOOKS

Nightboat Books, a nonprofit organization, seeks to develop audiences for writers whose work resists convention and transcends boundaries. We publish books rich with poignancy, intelligence, and risk. Please visit our website, www.nightboat.org, to learn about our titles and how you can support our future publications.

This book was made possible by a grant from the Topanga Fund, which is dedicated to promoting the arts and literature of California.

The following individuals have supported the publication of this book. We thank them for their generosity and commitment to the mission of Nightboat Books:

Kazim Ali
Elizabeth Motika
Chloe Silverman
Benjamin Taylor

This book has been made possible, in part, by a grant from the New York State Council on the Arts Literature Program.

NYSCA